—————— Fire ——————

Fire

POEMS BY

TIM 2 TAYLOR

TAYLOR PRODUCTIONS

JACKSONVILLE

——————— TIM 2 TAYLOR ———————

Copyright © 2018 by Tim Taylor Productions, Inc. All rights reserved.
This book in print, in digital e-publication, or audio or video formats may not
be copied or published in whole or in part without the prior written permission
of the author.

Copyright ©2018 by Tim Taylor

Fire - New Poems
First Printed Edition - 2018
First Digital Edition - 2018

Published by Tim Taylor Productions, Inc.
7536 Pottsburg Landing Drive
Jacksonville, Florida 32216

www.thefoundpoet.com
tim2taylor@facebook.com
Tim2.Taylor@instagram

Written by Tim 2 Taylor
Designed by Tim 2 Taylor
Edited by Tim 2 Taylor
Cover photography by Tim 2 Taylor

Library of Congress Control Number -

Taylor, Timothy, 1960 -

Manufactured in the United States
ISBN - 978-0-9833382-9-1 (book)
ISBN - 978-0-9833382-8-4 (e-book)

Printed copies by
Lightning Source Inc.
14 Ingram Blvd.
La Vergne, TN USA 37086
1. Poetry
Distributed by Tim Taylor Productions, Inc.
To purchase copies in bulk please contact: (904)-238-0889

To book Tim 2 Taylor for personal appearances, book signings or motivational
speaking engagements, please call (904) 238-0889 or contact Tim 2 through
the website at www.thefoundpoet.com

Be sure to read my other books: *The Found Poet- winter, The Found Poet- summer
and Wind* all available on Amazon.com or at your local bookstore.
Look for my weight-loss and fitness book *Fat As My Dad*
Watch for my new books "Life Loops™" and "Some Quotes"

2

Fire

*"I have found the fire
that can light the world
and conquer the darkness...
and it burns within each of us."*

− Tim 2 Taylor

TIM 2 TAYLOR

———— Fire ————

CONTENTS

PREFACE	7
Profound found invisible moment	9
Omikuji	11
Lighter	13
Carelessly dangling	15
The eruption	17
I want this	19
Relationship with time	21
The legends	23
The awakener	25
My woman	27
Of such a love	29
Night falls softly on us all	31
A mouth of blazing light	33
The rest is silence	35
Small tenderness	37
The floors of your heart	39
Love on the earth	41
This soft and fragile thing	43
I want	45
If you dare	47
Nothing but yours	49
I am round bread	51
Thirsty	53
Goosebumps	55
Reflection	57
Falling in grass with laughter	59
Bird Song	61
Rio	63
I'm longing to be	65

The question	67
Sneak away	69
Handful of hearts	71
The mare was gone	73
A simple puzzle snap	75
I never want to kiss you quickly	77
Bookmark	79
Tea ceremony	81
Junk Drawer	83
Bright morning face	85
Keys	87
Beach	89
Spring is near	91
Slip	93
Afford you tenderness	95
Wildly loved	97
EPILOGUE	99
About the author	100
Please write a review	101

Fire

PREFACE

Careful this book will ignite you. Poetry should always illuminate, warm and melt into your soul. It can also burn you to dark ash and smoke only to Phoenix re-birth you to glorious rising flames over and over.

This new collection of forty-four poems explores one of life's most powerful elements… Fire.

These poems move through the fiery feelings and emotions of fevered passions, scorching anger, consuming loss and the tender warmth of luminous love. Tim 2 explores the various natures of the fire within each of these emotions. As you read my words, my hope is that it helps you learn to meter the fire and embrace it's warmth without getting burned. That it allows you to walk through the fire and come out on the other side stronger and wiser.

Namaste

Tim 2 Taylor

Fire

Profound found invisible moment

You must hear me,
are you listening?
You must go out and be in it
in the morning
in this sacred moment

you must
stand in the mercy
of the rain to be wet
no slicker or bumpershoot
shielding of your tempered head
no big galoshes
bumbling upon your feet

stand in the whisper of it
to fall away with it
dance with it softly
allow the trickle to tickle
your smiling child's soul
for God's sake
you've been dry too damn long

splash
do you hear the glory of this word
splash in this wet forgiveness
leap up and land down
puddle deep jump
flowing between your toes
to remember your roots

laugh in resting the drops
see the truth of acceptance
that nothing in nature resist
everything cries out... rain on me
wash me clean, baptize me,
forget my dry sin
this second vanquished

profound found
invisible moment
that it is really this simple
to forgive yourself
forever washed away
out to the salty sea
where the shiny fish live

- Tim 2 Taylor

Fire

Omikuji

This morning
reverently crossing
the circular stones
islands amongst the pebbles

I leave my prayer
tied to a tree
to have the wind
blow warmly upon it

my hidden heart's desire
lashed to a branch
leaving my words
to bask in the golden sun

written by my own hand
soft linen offered up
bound to the tree's soul
holding it out to God's sky

like a sacred leaf
green in spirit
white in purity
heard yet unspoken

the small Shinto priest
nods approvingly my action
amplifying my dai-kichi,
(Great blessing)

Lighter

Am I lighter for the telling,
or from the being heard

does this lightness
come from bearing my truth

or from having you
gifting me acceptance

does this tiptoe dance
between us two a wafting feather

perhaps a folding cloth into
your arms of the night

a still kiss upon your palm
here in the morning

full a droplet rain upon us
lost within thunder

is it floating embers
flicking off desires flame

or the thirst to be
inside of you drifting away

abundantly I am lighter
so much lighter in love

──── Tim 2 Taylor ────

Carelessly dangling

I have come to fear
that I'm just another bangle
worn there upon your wrist
carelessly dangling
a mere flash
some past evidence
of being a shiny thing
that you once held
dear

———— TIM 2 TAYLOR ————

The eruption

Rumble rumble
scurry natives scurry
I don't want mere fire
I want volcano you
molten moving earth
deep beneath your surface
grinding tectonic passion
the length of me
touching the core of you
orange slow movement
unstoppable in its progression
overtaking and consuming
forming new earth
beneath our undulating bodies
pouring fire into your salty sea
steamy us dancing in the air
the shaking blast
the eruption
of such magnitude
the natives begin
looking for a virgin to toss

I want this

I awoke wanting you
my body laced to yours
lips melting upon the nape
of your neck lightly
my arms strong pulling you
towards white flagged surrender
and the weight of my body
resting with fire
my eyes walk through
the museum of your body
overtaken by its beauty
while my hands search
for a route like Vasco da Gama
oh to love you slowly
this morning of soft daybreak
to feast a breakfast of you
to please you purely
to love you deeply
to cuddle you to a smile
I want this

Relationship with time

Flame over this distance of time
together cupped against the flickering
of aged northern winds

so that we might feel

like old wizards
practicing ancient magic
embracing sparking fire
without turning to ash

like raw trembling teenagers
touching the heat of desire
blazingly un-hearthed

like old warriors speaking
of long ago battles
taking courage in our survival

like tiny finger-painters
exploring the feel of colors
squishy between fingers

like old lovers resting in
rocking chairs on the porch
of familiar comfort

you and I
and this rare
relationship with time

The legends

On my shore
Mermaid from the tide
oystered white pearl
resting softly ashore
the seven in your hair
with a mystic song voice
and a grander depth than
the distance to the moon
rolling pounding roar
your touch to heart
caught racing in my passing net
how could I ever toss
you back to sea
now that I know
the legends
are true

―――― Fire ――――

The awakener

I don't want to be a temptation
that pulls you to a darkened corner
never my love

I want to be an awakener
a bright lunged breath
raised in the morning

rousting lost things of long ago
shaking the slumbering life within you

calling loudly come be in this day
opened face to the sun
and walk loves golden path once more

knocking the dust off your resting tomes
of passions to read deeply of fiery unions kiss

bring you to remembrance of your heart's lyrics
and sing aloud dancing across laughters floor
softly spinning under mysterious stars

to stand in the rain wet again
with romance dripping from hair
and eyelashes

stirring the harvest pot
over an open flame and eat
this hearty meal warm bellied

lifting your spirit to float
in the blue like a child's
yellow kite wild fluttering
as hummingbird wings

oh my woman fair
curse me and put me away
for if I be a mere temptation
let me roll away from you as
blown smoke gray vanishing

for all I want to be is
your awakener this fine
morning.

――――― Fire ―――――

My woman

I wish to flow over your body
like golden wheat dancing
under the wind's soft touch

I yearn to hear you like the forest hears
the melting snows of winter,
trickling down mountain passes
plunging over waterfalls roar

I desire to lay in your arms
like the sunset pulls the nights covers
warmly over this spinning earth
starlit constellations crossing
heavens over us ebony complete

I long to kiss you
like the morning birds song
bright spirited, lilting constant,
full breasted, proudly joyous,
off the branch skyward soaring

I wish to turn to your smiling heart
like the sunflower rotates his face towards
the giving radiant orb washed in its light,
bathed in blissfulness, fully seen by the day

I want to be surrounded by you
like schools of great silvery fish
under salty depths shimmering
in warm vast currents a tide to every shore
washing enchanted

my woman
I must whisper these words
here upon your white skin
slowly into your broken heart open
for you to know my soul's voice
and the gentle nature of me

Of such a love

So many read the story
and never know your soul

storied holders of paragraphs,
verse or holy scripture

clinging to but a few chosen words
which I can understand, even cherish

but me

I want to read the loving face
hear the thundering voice
touch the very skin of the creator

of such a love
as yours

Fire

Night falls softly on us all

I'd forgotten
where the borders
of my heart were

the sharp edged barbed wire
long rusted away
fence post rotten to earth

the grand horses
on the great plains
free running

how could one consider
corralling them again
never, never

spirits of green and blue
skies as open
as their pumping hearts

this wind that blows
touching everything
seen and unseen

it is as it should be
the universe expands
with a kiss tender

and the horses vanish
over the distant horizon
and night falls softly on us all

A mouth of blazing light

My hand on the back
of your neck
lips diving to yours
meeting in a swirling
stirring offering
like the bow to the violin
to the strings pulled across
vibrating in my hands
restless sweetness
fills the air
unstoppable notes
this kiss soaring
lilting high
for I'm not kissing
a mere mortals lips
but the billionth star
found in the night sky
not faint or distant flickering
but a mouth of blazing light
an ages old beacon
that I sailor hath set upon
to sail his wondering way
home

The rest is silence

Do you know
that dew rests
petite in the morning
upon leaf green
and flower red

and that rain sits
fat on the day
rolling together
and cascading down
to dry earth

the water is the same
but how it comes
and goes is so different
this I've learned
from my own stillness

at this marvelous age
to become acute
of nature's simple ways
after so many days here
on this hastily spinning orb

the turning away from
this cage of mediocrity
the clanging chains of the many
my wings crisply open
in this blue sky

to become a renaissance man
of words and light
with great courage of heart
for religions speak of salvation,
then it is I who have surely found it

how long I resisted
my own clamoring heartbeat
held in imaginary fear
of unconcerned others
no longer, no not a minute more

I must speak now as nature
who rarely shouts
more in constant unison
with peace and persistence
and the rest is silence

―――― Fire ――――

Small tenderness

Your small tenderness
is like a log on my fire
on this cold winter day

It's the sunshine falling
through my window
resting upon my face
so uniquely warm

It's the constant sound
found down by the brook
a trickling over smooth pebbles
whispering confidence
in my ear

It's the brisk aroma
of coffee freshly poured
into my favorite mug
held in my hands

It's your morning kiss soft
leaving a smiling impression
within my heart

Yes... I love your small tenderness

The floors of your heart

There are days
that ebb distant
slowly flowing
days where I wish
I could sit at your window
peering in on your soul
seeing the inner workings
of your dancing life
learning intricate ways
knowing the comfort
of the furniture
that rest upon
the floors of your heart

——— Tim 2 Taylor ———

Fire

Love on the earth

The two
falling to the earth
like released leaves
from the sky

lightly resting
nestled amongst
the emerald grasses
and Italian red clay

giddy passion tumbling
hidden amongst the olive trees
the sounds of open kissing
a whisper of white lace

this magical spin of youth
the slipping of hands underneath clothes
and the wicked grass stains
that shall never come out

followed by your
spilling laughter
with hands running
like wild horses

the birds sing watching
this burning fire of eyes
all this beauty
all this innocent beauty

your small scream
is enough
to scatter the many wings
partaking of ripe olive meat

tussled hair with sweating smiles
and the staying in arms
knowing sweet tenderness of
love on the earth

This soft and fragile thing

I wish you understood
the balance you bring

the tenderness you carry
standing in my doorway

the missing pieces found
stolen so long ago

the torment you've put out to sea
destination unknown

the years of burning rust
your touch put a halt to

the breathing peace
back in my lungs full

you love... you have done this
soft and fragile thing

I want

I want to see your heart's needs
where others care not to look

I want to love you daily as if you are leaving
for a long overseas voyage

I want to care for you like the newborn
placed in a mothers' arms for the first time

I want to listen to you like a symphony,
bows to strings, lips to brass,
creating magic free in the air

I want to be amazed by you
like a child at the circus
three ring dazzled

I want to know you intimately
like an old sailor knows the winds
and the moving night sky

I want to laugh with you belly dropping
feet dangling roller coaster riding
hardy chuckles with unrestrained guffaws

I want to lay with you softy like
cotton clouds lay with the blue

I want to be close to you like gravity
is to the soles of my feet

I want these things
and altogether more,
for I am just a mere man
discovering what I want

Fire

If you dare

If you dare
come a little closer
see a little deeper me

If you're going to hum
this lively tune
you might as well sing

If you desire to read
my words
then by all means
read them out loud

If you care to dance
you must let your hand fly free
into this starry night

If you want my whiskey
ask for the damn bottle
and burn it down drunk

If you swim in my sea
come naked skinny dipping
leaping not timid treading

If you eat my food
be nourished well
satisfied napkin down

If you want to stay
stay because you're loved

not of your stealing need

If you kiss me tender
linger a few moments more
it will be worth it

If you truly love me
see a little deeper me
come a little closer
if you dare

Nothing but yours

Oh that I were free
loosed to love you
tender this day

unconfined lips
to speak, taste and kiss
your bright body fine

unbounded love
a roaming stallion
over your rolling plains

footloose passion
unbridled fiery desire
full within your velvet

unchained winds
to carefully caressing
those untouched places

a simple man who longs
for freedom to be
nothing but yours

Fire

I am round bread

Oh if I was a mere stone
satisfied to rest in the field
my soul to the earth
my face to the sun

but I am not a stone
I am round bread
oven fresh
every morning new

warm and soft
white and holy
with crisp golden
edges

I was meant to
nourish life
butter spread
savory

break me
woman
taste my heart
to fill thy belly

allow me to be
your sweet bread
resting here upon
your table

———— Tim 2 Taylor ————

Thirsty

If you come to me thirsty
I will pour you a glass of water

if you refuse to drink
please don't judge me

when you come again thirsty
to find the empty glass

it's not that I've quit pouring water,
it's that I'm giving it to those

who no longer wish
to be thirsty

Goosebumps

I once touched you lightly
roaming with tenderness
given in an honest instant
causing goosebumps to appear
upon your white wilderness
a sensual braille
to be blindly read softly
of a sweet story told
of a place reached within
of a quiet pleasure pure
of a connection rare and fine
though all too fleeting
spoke volumes to my heart
bringing a stirred wry smile
to my lips of desire
and a tremble
to my reading hand

Tim 2 Taylor

Fire

Reflection

You stood behind me
almost hiding
from the reflection
like me
until your embrace
still
then you ask me
to look at myself
broken open
blind no longer
the colors for the first time
suddenly for the briefest of moments
I felt beautiful
accepted
whole
shameless
and pure
in your arms safe
naked and strong
finally me
loving what I saw
in the mirror

Falling in grass with laughter

Tenderly my voice
slips into your ear
I pull up a chair
to sit comfortably
with your heart
to speak the words of my soul
fearlessly touching you
with a tone soft and somber
only to lay next to you
still knowing the breath
within your lungs
I'll be the white willow bark
holding to the tree of you
my skin must become your skin
of crushed velvet and dancing snow
my body's whispered poetry
moving you towards the dreams
of your innocent youth
a frolicking girl cartwheeling
falling in grass with laughter
and being genuinely in love

Bird Song

They come like a wave to shore
just before sunrise
with their winged chorus
of chipper happiness

Resting in the church
of my branches
full of morning praise
their joy of the coming light
uncontainable

The ecstasy and potential
to be found in the cresting day
a must sung melody of
the tinged blue overtaking
the black yet again

It washes on the beach
of my own stillness
lifted on this great tide of
whistled blessed contentment

I pray, I pray, I pray

Slowly they are off to their day
wings unfastened, chest out
taking to this vast sky which
beckons to us all

Rio

My golden skinned
friend lead me twisting
to the small hidden holes
where the heart of Rio
was unapologetically beating

the music played raw vibrant,
carefree so seductive

the kind of music that
rolls into your bones
instigating the wiggle
inherent to children

this was why I came
for I needed to touch
the unheard fire
born of smiles and drums

suddenly swept
into the dancing we
jangled arms and legs
souls and spirits
shaken and stirred

she leaned in close
to ask if I was happy
as if my face could
some how tell a lie

as if the peel of my smile
or sparkle in my eye
my serious joy
wasn't self evident

———— Fire ————

I'm longing to be

Sometimes I wish
I could wonder writing
in Walden woods like Thoreau

Or shoot the open
detailed grandness
of mountains like Ansel

Perhaps lift a brush to canvas
capturing the erotic nature
of flowers like O'keeffe

Write a sentence so powerful
of a peace found on a blue pond
with a white heron like Oliver

Sing a heartfelt Irish song
of a faith ripe with moving
love like Morrison

Maybe speak of the knowing
the curvy beauty of loving
a nude woman like Neruda

Their blood in me
many times I have wadded
into these waters
and sat at this table feasting

Still everyday
I'm longing to be
more

The question

See through my transparent skin
past my sinew and sin
past my bones of insecurity
to my red colored organ
my never muted heart pumping life blood

Feel the sexuality of creation
this Congo drum of rhythm
that moves me to dancing close
native sweat that runs
fingers through wet hair
aware of your Havana hips swinging free

See through these lungs
full of hot night air nostalgic and white
catch the glimpse of this slight smile
that has overcome lips awaiting your kiss
sweet mover of mountains

The body needs shaking from time to time
to be reminded that there is more
to being than slow routine
and swift tics of the clock
to recall the blind leaping of youth
burning, burning, burning

Can you feel this trembling truth?
Have you forgotten the answer?
Or worse have you forgotten to ask
the question?

Sneak away

Sneak away with me
let's escape
the bonds of this
ticky-tacky day
and it's imaginary importance
let's slip away
and make some permanence
drive down the winding country road
to that old watering hole
where we can giggle and wiggle
out of our useless clothes
and throw our naked bodies into it
alive swimming free
your eyes about my blue
I will kiss you like it's
a matter of life and death
and the catfish will purr
and blush at our love

Handful of hearts

I listen
only to hear
the beat of it

for it's a seldom thing
hearing another's heart
fresh and soft

even rarer
to be allowed in
utterly accepted

my darlings
we hold but a
handful of hearts

and carefully
powerfully,
another holds ours

on this pure day
I remember
a heartbeat

clear in rhythm
unlocking the door
of sweetest freedoms

opened for me
to walk through
born anew

how I cherish
the hearts
I hold dear

Fire

The mare was gone

I met her
on a sunshine plain
under the indigo
one rare day

she came without fear
of a lanky stranger
for she had stood
this ground long before I

noticing her eyes deep
looking through mine
her mane tasseled
by this smooth wind

burning light glistened
upon her body
as she wondered
about who I am

gingerly she stepped
to the heart of my chest
my hand simply flowed
across her neck pure

two spirits aware
we walked together
towards no place particular
she carried a steady pace to her stride
still one I could peacefully

match step for step

the things we shared
tremulous and true
an innate movement
like breathing

so near, yet so far
foretelling a distance
that couldn't
be covered by two

A cloud cast a shadow
the pull of her own life calls
here in a slow moment
the mare was gone

I stood alone
watching her vanish
into the horizon
somehow a tinge sadder
yet far richer man

Fire

A simple puzzle snap

He closed his red eyes
not being able to cry
about it any longer
and thought about
the little places
where the two of them
used to fit together
so easily... perfectly
a simple puzzle snap
of open laughter and quick passion
of soft kisses and tangled innocence
of holding hands and serious love songs
of words with meaning and looks of depth
his puzzled heart searched
for the rounded pieces
that could no longer
be found upon her table

I never want to kiss you quickly

I never want to kiss you quickly
no peckish meeting
nor airy Parisian kiss

how could I come
your tiny church doors
to the altar of your lips
and not pray slowly
revealing my heart's intent

thy sweet rose petals
I must breathe in deeply
linger like the bees crawling search
for craved nectar

for to kiss you quickly
would be blasphemous
a turn against nature itself

your two piano keys nestled
together making luscious hymns to affection
that must reverberate
upon my mouth

two robins eggs smooth resting
in the nest of your mouth
waiting for my feathered lips
to come and hatch into life

I never want to kiss you quickly

Bookmark

I've written you a soft letter
of sorrowful goodbye
for I'm not off to war
or leaving on a jet plane

It's that I can't pretend
I matter to you anymore
for I'm just a bookmark
between yellowing pages
of a book you shelved
years ago

and while you fondly
remember the deep words
you have no intention
of reading this book
ever again

Tea ceremony

The kettle's whistle
a gentle call to connection
potted tea steeping
for I desire
to bring you to warmth
    inside
seated across from you
our ceremony of stillness
the remembrance
of ancient things
the pouring out and in
the turn of a red cup
sipped across lips
this slowly shared
    intimacy
our love timeless
evergreen tea
moving us tenderly
together in this moment
a souls drink

Junk Drawer

I love rummaging around
in your junk drawer
surveying all
the assorted odds and ends

my fingers toddling
over curiosities,
until I come across
a trinket or treasure
that is uniquely you

oh I may play with it,
or love the feel of it
small in my hand
I might slip it into my pocket
and take it home

but more than likely
I'll place it back
in the junk drawer
so I can find it again
another day

Fire

Bright morning face

She makes an
awakening sound
so uniquely hers
like the distant roosters
righteous morning crow
twisted tucked in cotton covers
a smile is the first thing upon her face
even before her sparking eyes
pop freshly open
my lips are the second thing
upon her bright morning face

Keys

In my aging days
I've learned to love
without the need
for shackles of iron
but to love with keys
of gold instead

Beach

I had forgotten the feeling of being
so little against the vast horizon
seeing the straight edge before me
toes upon the soft sand

too long since I have stood
where the earth meets the great sea
sky gently waving her good mornings
greeting the warm rising orange orb
to move into the blue

submerged silent bubbles
this saltiness heals
a true baptism sinner to saint
to be once again like the fishes
buoyantly carefree

neck deep in an undulating mirror
of the sky above
lifting my soul free
no longer touching the bottom

Fire

Spring is near

If only you could see
your life as a garden,
how beautiful would it be

Wake up!
Wake up!
the feathered ones call

See the sun shining
on all this beautiful
chaos

Do you not have dirt
with access to seed
rain and rays?

Tell me what then,
what can be your
thin excuse?

Grow your beautiful!
Plant your seeds!
Sun your face!

The gentle
earth is turning
do you feel it?

spring is near

Fire

Slip

Oh this dream
sweet, sweet
awakened to want
this woman

I edge away the night
listening to your
slumbering breath
touching skin

drawn moth like
fluttering into
the flame of you
soft and curved
still and sleeping

to slowly rise
my body over yours
to rest upon your glorious earth beneath me

my flower
of the morning
who opens tenderly
with sunlight's cascade
upon thy dewed petals

allowing me to slip
into this moment
this body insatiable
inside love being born

fold me like a letter
of tearful love
into the envelope
of delivery

awaken to everything
everything worth finding
wrap your legs around
the truth of this day

hold to this stallion
ride across the plains
barebacked winded
towards our common destination

scream my love
scream yourself alive
shouting away the darkness
thy throat's sweet song of freedom

flutter downward tiny
like snow to the peace
in the valley below
whitely quiet

and hold this within
until our last breath
leaves us intertwined
eternally loved

Afford you tenderness

What could I speak
to change this past
tell me the words
I could write to change
the sea from the shore

Impossible

My darling there is no key
for a door that doesn't exist
in my youth I built strong walls
now old I'll never lay another stone

I've learned to not dance
with dry jangle bones
as no spell can conjure
new sinew and flesh

hear me speak love
for I am not wealthy
nor do I have all
the grand answers

but I can pray and love
and afford you tenderness
if you could only understand
this truly is enough
for us to live

Wildly loved

It's never found
in the past

nor reachable
in the future

it's everything found
in this very rich moment

so breathe...
knowing you are

still, free and
wildly loved

EPILOGUE

Fire. This beautiful fire called life. I hope this book has warmed your heart and made you feel this sacred fire. For so long I refused to deal with the fire of my life. Either it was raging out of control or a slight flicker left unattended.

I'd been afraid to get close to my personal flame. Afraid to get burned. I wrote this poem for my upcoming "Quotes" book:

> "There is no better teacher
> of the dangers of fire
> than one who has just been burned.
> Unless you yourself are on fire."

Several years ago my spirit caught fire and I started writing my poetry. I've been burned for sure, but the illumination, the warmth, the love have been so worth it.

Let me encourage you to reach for your own fire. Find your own passion. Let it ignite your heart. Stoke the fires of actually living your life for you! Burn. For life is about the burning.

Peace
Peace
Peace

Tim 2 Taylor

About the author

Tim 2 Taylor, was a child of the 60's growing up in the slow paced, redneck turbulent south on the outskirts of Atlanta, Georgia. He struggled through the school years as he suffered with undiagnosed dyslexia. A teenage girlfriend gave him his first book of poetry *"The Prophet"* by Kahlil Gibran, which awakened a passion for writing. After graduating, he married his junior high school sweetheart and moved to Florida. Sadly, the marriage ended two years later.

As an adult, Taylor remarried and started a career in advertising. He worked at several nationally ranked agencies as an art director and creative director. Taylor opened his own successful agency 25 years ago -Taylor Productions Inc.
He recently launched his second company - Fat As My Dad, LLC.

At the age of 45, Taylor flat lined in the back of an ambulance. Having a near death experience only to be revived, he got a second chance at life. Hence the "2" in his name representing the "2nd " life he's living now.

Within a year he lost 99 pounds and was selected USA Today's 2007 Weight-loss champion and reshaped his life forever.

Currently Tim 2 is a nationally recognized motivational health and fitness speaker and life coach, featured in magazines, radio and TV shows. He is the author of the fitness and weight-loss book *"Fat As My Dad."*

In recent years Tim 2 has rediscovered his passion for writing poetry. He's written three other books of poetry: *"The Found Poet - summer", "The Found Poet - winter"* and *"Wind".*

Taylor is also a renowned, award winning nature and flower photographer.

www.thefoundpoet.com • Instagram: @tim2.taylor

Please write a review

If you enjoyed this book please be sure to write a five star review at Amazon.com. In today's book selling marketplace reviews are so important. I really love hearing what people think about my work and by writing a review you can let your voice be heard.

You can find my other books on Amazon or at your local bookstore as well.

You can also purchase my merchandise at my website:
www.squareup.com/journytobeauty

Thanks in advance!

Follow me on Facebook
Tim Taylor
and
Tim 2 Taylor

On Instagram at:
Tim2.Taylor

——— Tim 2 Taylor ———

www.ingramcontent.com/pod-product-compliance
Lightning Source LLC
Chambersburg PA
CBHW031356160426
42813CB00082B/403